Addition Facts 1-6

D1358805

The answer to an addition problem is called the **sum**.
You write the **equation** like this: **2 + 3 = 5**

$$\underline{}2\underline{} + \underline{}3\underline{} = \underline{}5\underline{}$$

Write the **equations** for the addition problems.

1. 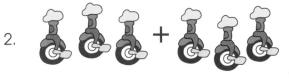   _____ + _____ = _____

2.    _____ + _____ = _____

3.    _____ + _____ = _____

4.    _____ + _____ = _____

5.    _____ + _____ = _____

6.    _____ + _____ = _____

7.    _____ + _____ = _____

More Addition Facts 1-6

Try using this number line to find
the **sum** to the equation **4 + 2**.
Start at **4**. Count forward **2** numbers. That's your answer!

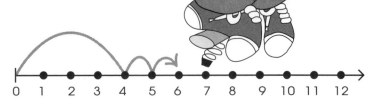

The **sum** of **4 + 2** is **6**.

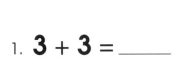

Find the **sum** to each equation. Use the number line for help.

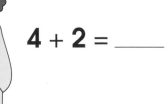

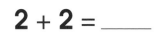

1. **3 + 3 = ____**   **1 + 4 = ____**   **4 + 2 = ____**

2. **5 + 1 = ____**   **2 + 3 = ____**   **2 + 2 = ____**

3.
$$\begin{array}{r} 4 \\ +1 \\ \hline \end{array} \qquad \begin{array}{r} 2 \\ +4 \\ \hline \end{array} \qquad \begin{array}{r} 3 \\ +3 \\ \hline \end{array} \qquad \begin{array}{r} 1 \\ +1 \\ \hline \end{array} \qquad \begin{array}{r} 5 \\ +0 \\ \hline \end{array}$$

4.
$$\begin{array}{r} 2 \\ +2 \\ \hline \end{array} \qquad \begin{array}{r} 1 \\ +2 \\ \hline \end{array} \qquad \begin{array}{r} 4 \\ +0 \\ \hline \end{array} \qquad \begin{array}{r} 3 \\ +2 \\ \hline \end{array} \qquad \begin{array}{r} 1 \\ +3 \\ \hline \end{array}$$

Subtraction Facts 1-6

The answer to a subtraction equation is called the **difference**.
The equation for this picture is: **4 – 2 = 2**.

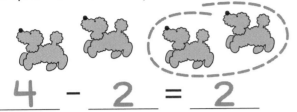

$$\underline{4} - \underline{2} = \underline{2}$$

Write the equations for the **subtraction** problems.

1.    _____ – _____ = _____

2.    _____ – _____ = _____

3.    _____ – _____ = _____

4.    _____ – _____ = _____

5.    _____ – _____ = _____

6.    _____ – _____ = _____

7.    _____ – _____ = _____

More Subtraction Facts 1 - 6

Try using this number line to find the **difference** to the equation **6 - 4**. Start at **6**. Count back **4** numbers. That's your answer!

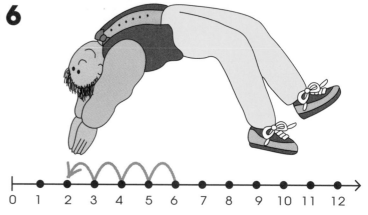

The **difference** of 6 - 4 is 2.

Find the **difference** to each equation. Use the number line for help.

1. **6 - 3 = _____**   **5 - 2 = _____**   **4 - 2 = _____**

2. **3 - 2 = _____**   **3 - 1 = _____**   **2 - 1 = _____**

3.
$$5 - 1$$ $$6 - 4$$

4.
$$5 - 0$$ $$4 - 2$$ $$6 - 3$$ $$6 - 5$$

5.
$$5 - 2$$ $$4 - 3$$ $$3 - 2$$ $$4 - 0$$

Family of Facts 1 – 6

A **family of facts** uses the **same numbers**.
Meet the family of **5**.

$$3 + 2 = 5$$
$$2 + 3 = 5$$
$$5 - 2 = 3$$
$$5 - 3 = 2$$

Find the answers for each **fact family**.

1.
$$\begin{array}{r} 3 \\ + 3 \\ \hline \end{array} \qquad \begin{array}{r} 6 \\ - 3 \\ \hline \end{array}$$

2.
$$\begin{array}{r} 1 \\ + 1 \\ \hline \end{array} \qquad \begin{array}{r} 2 \\ - 1 \\ \hline \end{array}$$

3.
$$\begin{array}{r} 2 \\ + 2 \\ \hline \end{array} \qquad \begin{array}{r} 4 \\ - 2 \\ \hline \end{array}$$

4.
$$\begin{array}{r} 5 \\ + 1 \\ \hline \end{array} \qquad \begin{array}{r} 1 \\ + 5 \\ \hline \end{array} \qquad \begin{array}{r} 6 \\ - 5 \\ \hline \end{array} \qquad \begin{array}{r} 6 \\ - 1 \\ \hline \end{array}$$

5.
$$\begin{array}{r} 4 \\ + 2 \\ \hline \end{array} \qquad \begin{array}{r} 2 \\ + 4 \\ \hline \end{array} \qquad \begin{array}{r} 6 \\ - 4 \\ \hline \end{array} \qquad \begin{array}{r} 6 \\ - 2 \\ \hline \end{array}$$

6.
$$\begin{array}{r} 1 \\ + 3 \\ \hline \end{array} \qquad \begin{array}{r} 3 \\ + 1 \\ \hline \end{array} \qquad \begin{array}{r} 4 \\ - 1 \\ \hline \end{array} \qquad \begin{array}{r} 4 \\ - 3 \\ \hline \end{array}$$

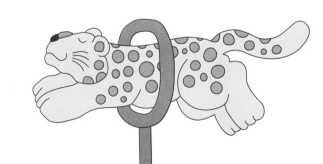

Adding and Subtracting 0 and 1

$0 + 0 = 0$
$1 + 0 = 1$
$2 + 0 = 2$ $1 + 1 = 2$
$3 + 0 = 3$ $2 + 1 = 3$
$4 + 0 = 4$ $3 + 1 = 4$
$5 + 0 = 5$ $4 + 1 = 5$
$6 + 0 = 6$ $5 + 1 = 6$

$0 - 0 = 0$
$1 - 0 = 1$ $1 - 1 = 0$
$2 - 0 = 2$ $2 - 1 = 1$
$3 - 0 = 3$ $3 - 1 = 2$
$4 - 0 = 4$ $4 - 1 = 3$
$5 - 0 = 5$ $5 - 1 = 4$
$6 - 0 = 6$ $6 - 1 = 5$

Find the **sums**.

1.
$$\begin{array}{r} 4 \\ +\,0 \\ \hline \end{array} \qquad \begin{array}{r} 2 \\ +\,1 \\ \hline \end{array} \qquad \begin{array}{r} 5 \\ +\,1 \\ \hline \end{array} \qquad \begin{array}{r} 1 \\ +\,4 \\ \hline \end{array} \qquad \begin{array}{r} 2 \\ +\,0 \\ \hline \end{array}$$

2.
$$\begin{array}{r} 4 \\ +\,2 \\ \hline \end{array} \qquad \begin{array}{r} 3 \\ +\,3 \\ \hline \end{array} \qquad \begin{array}{r} 2 \\ +\,3 \\ \hline \end{array} \qquad \begin{array}{r} 1 \\ +\,3 \\ \hline \end{array} \qquad \begin{array}{r} 3 \\ +\,2 \\ \hline \end{array}$$

Find the **differences**.

3.
$$\begin{array}{r} 3 \\ -\,1 \\ \hline \end{array} \qquad \begin{array}{r} 2 \\ -\,1 \\ \hline \end{array} \qquad \begin{array}{r} 4 \\ -\,1 \\ \hline \end{array} \qquad \begin{array}{r} 3 \\ -\,0 \\ \hline \end{array} \qquad \begin{array}{r} 1 \\ -\,1 \\ \hline \end{array}$$

4.
$$\begin{array}{r} 5 \\ -\,3 \\ \hline \end{array} \qquad \begin{array}{r} 5 \\ -\,4 \\ \hline \end{array} \qquad \begin{array}{r} 0 \\ -\,0 \\ \hline \end{array} \qquad \begin{array}{r} 4 \\ -\,4 \\ \hline \end{array} \qquad \begin{array}{r} 3 \\ -\,2 \\ \hline \end{array}$$

More Adding and Subtracting

Write the **sum** or **difference**.

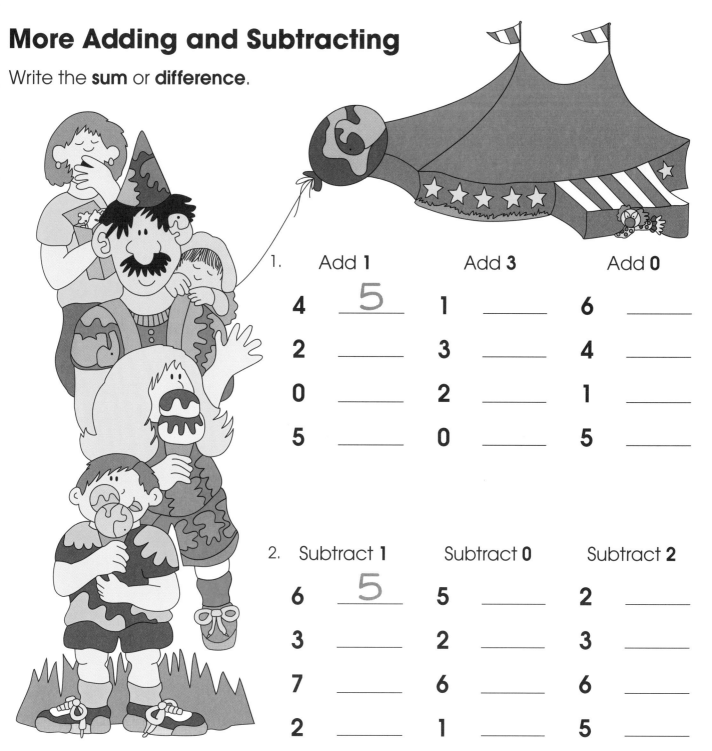

1.

	Add **1**		Add **3**		Add **0**
4	5	1	_____	6	_____
2	_____	3	_____	4	_____
0	_____	2	_____	1	_____
5	_____	0	_____	5	_____

2.

	Subtract **1**		Subtract **0**		Subtract **2**
6	5	5	_____	2	_____
3	_____	2	_____	3	_____
7	_____	6	_____	6	_____
2	_____	1	_____	5	_____

How many hidden elephants can you find in the picture?
Finish the table to find the answer.

2	+ 4		− 3		− 1		+ 2	=	

Elephants

Addition Facts 7 and 8

Pictures can help us learn facts!

Write the equations for the **addition** problems.

1. _____ + _____ = _____

2. _____ + _____ = _____

3. _____ + _____ = _____

4. _____ + _____ = _____

5. _____ + _____ = _____

6. _____ + _____ = _____

7. _____ + _____ = _____

Subtraction Facts 7 and 8

Write the equations for the **subtraction** problems.

1.  $\underline{7} - \underline{5} = \underline{2}$

2. $\underline{\hphantom{0}} - \underline{\hphantom{0}} = \underline{\hphantom{0}}$

3. $\underline{\hphantom{0}} - \underline{\hphantom{0}} = \underline{\hphantom{0}}$

4. $\underline{\hphantom{0}} - \underline{\hphantom{0}} = \underline{\hphantom{0}}$

5. $\underline{\hphantom{0}} - \underline{\hphantom{0}} = \underline{\hphantom{0}}$

6. $\underline{\hphantom{0}} - \underline{\hphantom{0}} = \underline{\hphantom{0}}$

7. $\underline{\hphantom{0}} - \underline{\hphantom{0}} = \underline{\hphantom{0}}$

Practice Facts 7 and 8

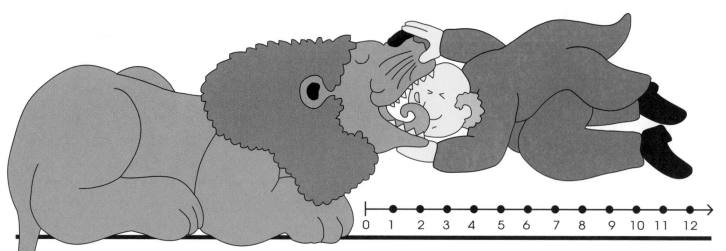

Find the **sum** or **difference** for each equation.

1. $4 + 3 = \underline{\hspace{1cm}}$ $6 + 2 = \underline{\hspace{1cm}}$ $8 - 4 = \underline{\hspace{1cm}}$

2. $8 - 3 = \underline{\hspace{1cm}}$ $1 + 6 = \underline{\hspace{1cm}}$ $7 - 4 = \underline{\hspace{1cm}}$

3. $2 + 5 = \underline{\hspace{1cm}}$ $7 + 1 = \underline{\hspace{1cm}}$ $8 - 2 = \underline{\hspace{1cm}}$

4.
$$\begin{array}{r} 6 \\ + 2 \\ \hline \end{array} \qquad \begin{array}{r} 7 \\ - 2 \\ \hline \end{array} \qquad \begin{array}{r} 0 \\ + 7 \\ \hline \end{array} \qquad \begin{array}{r} 8 \\ - 2 \\ \hline \end{array} \qquad \begin{array}{r} 8 \\ - 5 \\ \hline \end{array}$$

5.
$$\begin{array}{r} 7 \\ - 5 \\ \hline \end{array} \qquad \begin{array}{r} 8 \\ - 3 \\ \hline \end{array} \qquad \begin{array}{r} 5 \\ + 3 \\ \hline \end{array} \qquad \begin{array}{r} 7 \\ - 3 \\ \hline \end{array} \qquad \begin{array}{r} 4 \\ + 4 \\ \hline \end{array}$$

Family of Facts 7 and 8

$5 + 3 = 8$ $3 + 5 = 8$ $8 - 5 = 3$ $8 - 3 = 5$

Find the answers for each **fact family**.

1.
$$\begin{array}{r} 4 \\ +3 \\ \hline \end{array} \qquad \begin{array}{r} 3 \\ +4 \\ \hline \end{array} \qquad \begin{array}{r} 7 \\ -4 \\ \hline \end{array} \qquad \begin{array}{r} 7 \\ -3 \\ \hline \end{array}$$

2.
$$\begin{array}{r} 7 \\ +0 \\ \hline \end{array} \qquad \begin{array}{r} 7 \\ -0 \\ \hline \end{array}$$

3.
$$\begin{array}{r} 4 \\ +4 \\ \hline \end{array} \qquad \begin{array}{r} 8 \\ -4 \\ \hline \end{array}$$

4.
$$\begin{array}{r} 2 \\ +5 \\ \hline \end{array} \qquad \begin{array}{r} 5 \\ +2 \\ \hline \end{array} \qquad \begin{array}{r} 7 \\ -2 \\ \hline \end{array} \qquad \begin{array}{r} 7 \\ -5 \\ \hline \end{array}$$

5.
$$\begin{array}{r} 2 \\ +6 \\ \hline \end{array} \qquad \begin{array}{r} 6 \\ +2 \\ \hline \end{array} \qquad \begin{array}{r} 8 \\ -2 \\ \hline \end{array} \qquad \begin{array}{r} 8 \\ -6 \\ \hline \end{array}$$

6.
$$\begin{array}{r} 7 \\ +1 \\ \hline \end{array} \qquad \begin{array}{r} 1 \\ +7 \\ \hline \end{array} \qquad \begin{array}{r} 8 \\ -7 \\ \hline \end{array} \qquad \begin{array}{r} 8 \\ -1 \\ \hline \end{array}$$

7.
$$\begin{array}{r} 8 \\ +0 \\ \hline \end{array} \qquad \begin{array}{r} 8 \\ -0 \\ \hline \end{array}$$

Addition Facts 9 and 10

Write the equations for the **addition** problems.

1. ____ + ____ = ____

2. ____ + ____ = ____

3. ____ + ____ = ____

4. ____ + ____ = ____

5. ____ + ____ = ____

6. ____ + ____ = ____

7. ____ + ____ = ____

Subtraction Facts 9 and 10

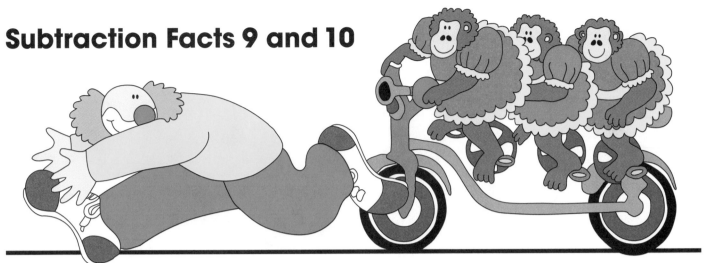

Write the equations for the **subtraction** problems.

1. 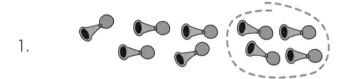   _____ – _____ = _____

2.   _____ – _____ = _____

3.   _____ – _____ = _____

4.   _____ – _____ = _____

5.   _____ – _____ = _____

6.   _____ – _____ = _____

7.   _____ – _____ = _____

Family of Facts 9 and 10

$$8 + 1 = 9$$
$$1 + 8 = 9$$
$$9 - 8 = 1$$
$$9 - 1 = 8$$

Find the answers for each **fact family**.

1. $\begin{array}{r} 6 \\ +3 \\ \hline \end{array}$ $\begin{array}{r} 3 \\ +6 \\ \hline \end{array}$ $\begin{array}{r} 9 \\ -6 \\ \hline \end{array}$ $\begin{array}{r} 9 \\ -3 \\ \hline \end{array}$

2. $\begin{array}{r} 5 \\ +4 \\ \hline \end{array}$ $\begin{array}{r} 4 \\ +5 \\ \hline \end{array}$ $\begin{array}{r} 9 \\ -5 \\ \hline \end{array}$ $\begin{array}{r} 9 \\ -4 \\ \hline \end{array}$

3. $\begin{array}{r} 6 \\ +4 \\ \hline \end{array}$ $\begin{array}{r} 4 \\ +6 \\ \hline \end{array}$ $\begin{array}{r} 10 \\ -6 \\ \hline \end{array}$ $\begin{array}{r} 10 \\ -4 \\ \hline \end{array}$

4. $\begin{array}{r} 7 \\ +3 \\ \hline \end{array}$ $\begin{array}{r} 3 \\ +7 \\ \hline \end{array}$ $\begin{array}{r} 10 \\ -7 \\ \hline \end{array}$ $\begin{array}{r} 10 \\ -3 \\ \hline \end{array}$

5. $\begin{array}{r} 2 \\ +8 \\ \hline \end{array}$ $\begin{array}{r} 8 \\ +2 \\ \hline \end{array}$ $\begin{array}{r} 10 \\ -2 \\ \hline \end{array}$ $\begin{array}{r} 10 \\ -8 \\ \hline \end{array}$

Practice Facts 9 and 10

Find the **sum** or **difference** for each equation.

1. $9 - 3 =$ _____ $4 + 5 =$ _____ $9 - 4 =$ _____

2. $5 + 5 =$ _____ $9 - 7 =$ _____ $10 - 2 =$ _____

3. $4 + 6 =$ _____ $10 - 4 =$ _____ $7 + 2 =$ _____

4.
$$\begin{array}{r} 7 \\ + 3 \\ \hline \end{array} \qquad \begin{array}{r} 8 \\ + 2 \\ \hline \end{array} \qquad \begin{array}{r} 9 \\ - 0 \\ \hline \end{array}$$

5.
$$\begin{array}{r} 9 \\ - 6 \\ \hline \end{array} \qquad \begin{array}{r} 9 \\ - 2 \\ \hline \end{array} \qquad \begin{array}{r} 3 \\ + 7 \\ \hline \end{array}$$

6.
$$\begin{array}{r} 6 \\ + 4 \\ \hline \end{array} \qquad \begin{array}{r} 10 \\ - 5 \\ \hline \end{array} \qquad \begin{array}{r} 9 \\ - 1 \\ \hline \end{array}$$

Addition and Subtraction Practice 1 - 10

Find the **sum** or **difference** for each equation.

10 − 7 = _____   ★2 + 8 = _____

Ladder 1

$$0 \atop + 4$$

$$9 \atop - 2$$

$$10 \atop - 8$$

$$9 \atop - 3$$

$$3 \atop + 4$$

$$6 \atop + 3$$

5 + 4 = _____

3 + 5 = _____

6 + 4 = _____

10 − 2 = _____

8 − 5 = _____

It's beary easy!

Ladder 2

$$7 \atop + 3$$

$$10 \atop - 0$$

$$5 \atop + 2$$

$$9 \atop - 6$$

$$4 \atop + 4$$

$$7 \atop + 2$$

Practice Facts 1-10

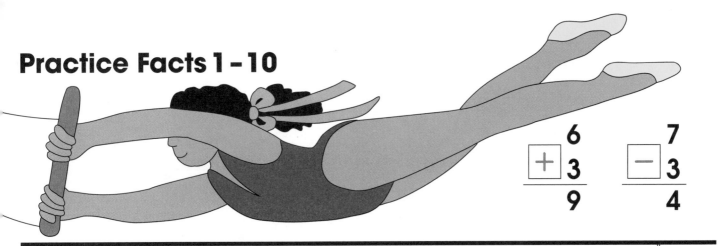

$$\begin{array}{r} 6 \\ +\ 3 \\ \hline 9 \end{array} \qquad \begin{array}{r} 7 \\ -\ 3 \\ \hline 4 \end{array}$$

Fill in the blanks to make the equations true using a **+** or **−** sign.

1.
$$\begin{array}{r}5\\ \square\ 5\\ \hline 10\end{array} \qquad \begin{array}{r}6\\ \square\ 2\\ \hline 4\end{array} \qquad \begin{array}{r}5\\ \square\ 3\\ \hline 2\end{array} \qquad \begin{array}{r}8\\ \square\ 2\\ \hline 10\end{array}$$

2.
$$\begin{array}{r}8\\ \square\ 5\\ \hline 3\end{array} \qquad \begin{array}{r}2\\ \square\ 6\\ \hline 8\end{array} \qquad \begin{array}{r}6\\ \square\ 4\\ \hline 2\end{array} \qquad \begin{array}{r}7\\ \square\ 1\\ \hline 6\end{array}$$

3.
$$\begin{array}{r}6\\ \square\ 3\\ \hline 9\end{array} \qquad \begin{array}{r}9\\ \square\ 4\\ \hline 5\end{array} \qquad \begin{array}{r}8\\ \square\ 6\\ \hline 2\end{array} \qquad \begin{array}{r}2\\ \square\ 5\\ \hline 7\end{array}$$

4.
$$\begin{array}{r}2\\ \square\ 6\\ \hline 8\end{array} \qquad \begin{array}{r}9\\ \square\ 5\\ \hline 4\end{array} \qquad \begin{array}{r}7\\ \square\ 4\\ \hline 3\end{array} \qquad \begin{array}{r}4\\ \square\ 6\\ \hline 10\end{array}$$

It's not as hard as it looks!

Fact Families of 11

Work on these facts for the family of **11**.
There are **12** lions. Use them as a number line if you need help.

1. | 2 | 9 | 11 | 11 |
    |+9|+2|− 2|− 9|

2. | 4 | 7 | 11 | 11 |
    |+7|+4|− 4|− 7|

3. | 10 | 1 | 11 | 11 |
    |+ 1|+10|−10|− 1|

4. | 5 | 6 | 11 | 11 |
    |+6|+5|− 5|− 6|

Fact Families of 12

Work on these facts for the family of **12**.

1.
$$\begin{array}{r} 4 \\ +8 \\ \hline \end{array} \qquad \begin{array}{r} 8 \\ +4 \\ \hline \end{array} \qquad \begin{array}{r} 12 \\ -4 \\ \hline \end{array} \qquad \begin{array}{r} 12 \\ -8 \\ \hline \end{array}$$

2.
$$\begin{array}{r} 9 \\ +3 \\ \hline \end{array} \qquad \begin{array}{r} 3 \\ +9 \\ \hline \end{array} \qquad \begin{array}{r} 12 \\ -9 \\ \hline \end{array} \qquad \begin{array}{r} 12 \\ -3 \\ \hline \end{array}$$

3.
$$\begin{array}{r} 11 \\ +1 \\ \hline \end{array} \qquad \begin{array}{r} 1 \\ +11 \\ \hline \end{array} \qquad \begin{array}{r} 12 \\ -11 \\ \hline \end{array} \qquad \begin{array}{r} 12 \\ -1 \\ \hline \end{array}$$

4.
$$\begin{array}{r} 5 \\ +7 \\ \hline \end{array} \qquad \begin{array}{r} 7 \\ +5 \\ \hline \end{array} \qquad \begin{array}{r} 12 \\ -5 \\ \hline \end{array} \qquad \begin{array}{r} 12 \\ -7 \\ \hline \end{array}$$

You charm
the skin off
me!

Practice Facts 1-12

Find the **sum** or **difference**.
Circle the clown with the **greatest** total.
He will jump into the bucket first.

10	4	12	0	7	5
+ 2	+ 7	− 8	+ 9	− 3	+ 2
− 6	− 6	− 4	+ 2	+ 8	− 4
− 3	+ 5	+ 5	− 7	− 4	− 2

Counting On to Add

Counting on helps you find the **sum** faster.
To **count on** start with the **greatest** number (**5**).
Count **3** numbers more (**5**), **6**, **7**, **8**. The **sum** is **8**.

$$5 + 3 = 8$$

| 0 | 1 | 2 | 3 | 4 | 5 | 6 | 7 | 8 | 9 | 10 | 11 | 12 |

Find the **sum** to each problem. **Count on** if you need help.

1. $8 + 3 =$ ____ $2 + 7 =$ ____ $5 + 5 =$ ____

2. $6 + 6 =$ ____ $9 + 2 =$ ____ $7 + 4 =$ ____

3. $11 + 1 =$ ____ $4 + 8 =$ ____ $3 + 5 =$ ____

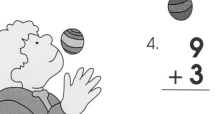

4.
$$\begin{array}{r} 9 \\ + 3 \\ \hline \end{array}$$
$$\begin{array}{r} 4 \\ + 4 \\ \hline \end{array}$$
$$\begin{array}{r} 7 \\ + 5 \\ \hline \end{array}$$

5.
$$\begin{array}{r} 5 \\ + 6 \\ \hline \end{array}$$
$$\begin{array}{r} 8 \\ + 2 \\ \hline \end{array}$$
$$\begin{array}{r} 6 \\ + 3 \\ \hline \end{array}$$

6.
$$\begin{array}{r} 4 \\ + 3 \\ \hline \end{array}$$
$$\begin{array}{r} 5 \\ + 4 \\ \hline \end{array}$$
$$\begin{array}{r} 6 \\ + 4 \\ \hline \end{array}$$

Counting Back to Subtract

Counting back helps you find the **difference** faster.
To **count back** start with the **greatest** number **(11)**.
Count **5** numbers back **(11)**, **10**, **9**, **8**, **7**, **6**. The **difference** is **6**.

$$11 - 5 = 6$$

| 0 | 1 | 2 | 3 | 4 | 5 | 6 | 7 | 8 | 9 | 10 | 11 | 12 |

Find the **difference** to each equation. **Count back** if you need help.

1. $12 - 7 = \underline{\hphantom{00}}$ $11 - 7 = \underline{\hphantom{00}}$ $10 - 8 = \underline{\hphantom{00}}$

2. $11 - 2 = \underline{\hphantom{00}}$ $10 - 2 = \underline{\hphantom{00}}$ $10 - 6 = \underline{\hphantom{00}}$

3. $12 - 5 = \underline{\hphantom{00}}$ $11 - 5 = \underline{\hphantom{00}}$

4.
$$\begin{array}{r} 12 \\ -\ 8 \\ \hline \end{array} \qquad \begin{array}{r} 11 \\ -\ 7 \\ \hline \end{array} \qquad \begin{array}{r} 10 \\ -\ 5 \\ \hline \end{array}$$

5.
$$\begin{array}{r} 12 \\ -\ 3 \\ \hline \end{array} \qquad \begin{array}{r} 9 \\ -\ 4 \\ \hline \end{array} \qquad \begin{array}{r} 11 \\ -\ 6 \\ \hline \end{array}$$

6.
$$\begin{array}{r} 12 \\ -\ 6 \\ \hline \end{array} \qquad \begin{array}{r} 12 \\ -\ 4 \\ \hline \end{array} \qquad \begin{array}{r} 12 \\ -\ 8 \\ \hline \end{array}$$

Practice Counting On and Counting Back

Find the **sum** or the **difference** and solve the riddle.
Use the code to find the answer.

Sometimes they call them kings.
At the circus they jump through rings.

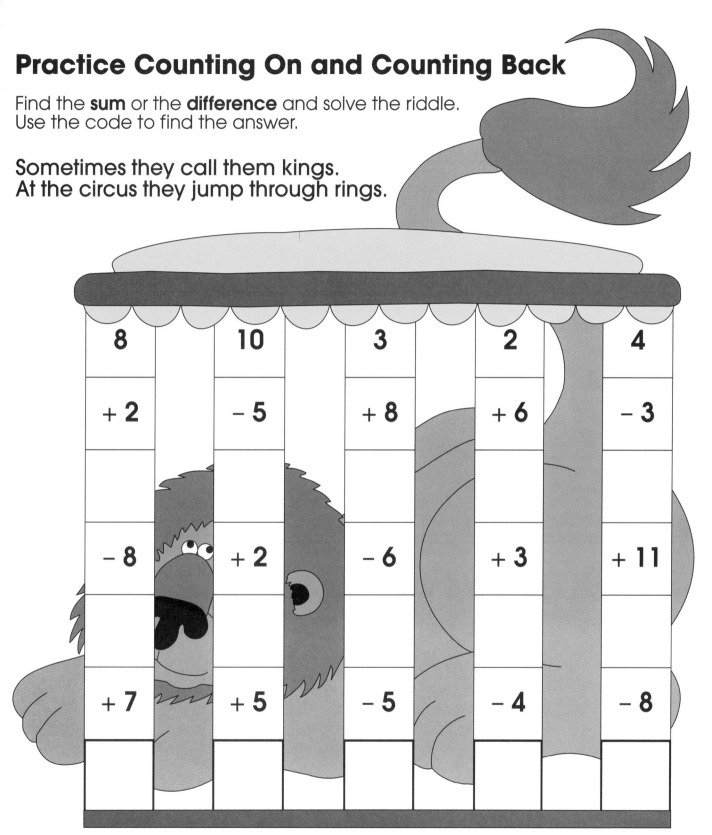

8	10	3	2	4
+ 2	− 5	+ 8	+ 6	− 3
− 8	+ 2	− 6	+ 3	+ 11
+ 7	+ 5	− 5	− 4	− 8

code

0	1	2	3	4	5	6	7	8	9	10	11	12
o	z	e	b	s	r	k	n	h	l	f	p	i

_____   _____   _____   _____

Adding Three Addends

To add three numerals (**addends**) together you:

1. Add the **5 + 4** and the **sum** is **9**.

2. Then add the **sum** of **9** to the **2** and the **sum** is **11**.

$$\left.\begin{array}{r} 5 \\ 4 \end{array}\right] = 9$$
$$\begin{array}{r} +\ 2 \\ \hline 11 \end{array}$$

Find the **sums**.

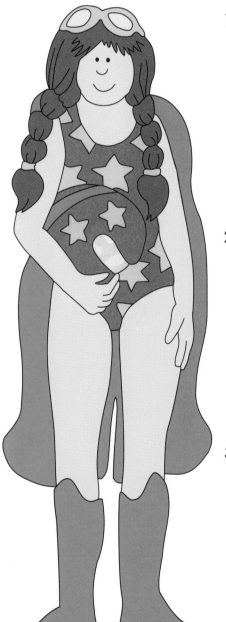

1.
$$\begin{array}{r} 2 \\ 6 \\ +\ 3 \\ \hline \end{array}$$
$$\begin{array}{r} 1 \\ 8 \\ +\ 3 \\ \hline \end{array}$$
$$\begin{array}{r} 9 \\ 1 \\ +\ 2 \\ \hline \end{array}$$
$$\begin{array}{r} 2 \\ 4 \\ +\ 5 \\ \hline \end{array}$$

2.
$$\begin{array}{r} 4 \\ 7 \\ +\ 1 \\ \hline \end{array}$$
$$\begin{array}{r} 4 \\ 4 \\ +\ 2 \\ \hline \end{array}$$
$$\begin{array}{r} 3 \\ 1 \\ +\ 7 \\ \hline \end{array}$$
$$\begin{array}{r} 5 \\ 5 \\ +\ 2 \\ \hline \end{array}$$

3.
$$\begin{array}{r} 6 \\ 2 \\ +\ 2 \\ \hline \end{array}$$
$$\begin{array}{r} 4 \\ 4 \\ +\ 4 \\ \hline \end{array}$$
$$\begin{array}{r} 3 \\ 2 \\ +\ 5 \\ \hline \end{array}$$
$$\begin{array}{r} 1 \\ 2 \\ +\ 8 \\ \hline \end{array}$$

Adding Tens and Ones

1. Add the **ones**.

```
  tens ones
    1   3
 +  4
    ___
        7
```

2. Add the **tens**.

```
  tens ones
    1   3
 +      4
    _____
    1   7
```

Add the **ones**.
Then add the **tens**.

1.

```
 tens ones
    6  3
 +     5
```

```
    9  1
 +     6
```

```
    5  0
 +     8
```

2.

```
    7  2
 +     1
```

```
    2  5
 +     3
```

```
    5  3
 +     6
```

3.

```
    4  5
 + 1  4
```

```
    2  7
 + 6  0
```

```
    4  4
 + 3  4
```

More Tens and Ones to Add

REMEMBER: Add the **ones** and then the **tens**!

1.
$$\begin{array}{r} 56 \\ + 20 \\ \hline \end{array}$$
$$\begin{array}{r} 71 \\ + 15 \\ \hline \end{array}$$
$$\begin{array}{r} 43 \\ + 32 \\ \hline \end{array}$$
$$\begin{array}{r} 20 \\ + 48 \\ \hline \end{array}$$

2.
$$\begin{array}{r} 81 \\ + 10 \\ \hline \end{array}$$
$$\begin{array}{r} 90 \\ + \ 7 \\ \hline \end{array}$$
$$\begin{array}{r} 85 \\ + 13 \\ \hline \end{array}$$
$$\begin{array}{r} 34 \\ + 35 \\ \hline \end{array}$$

3.
$$\begin{array}{r} 20 \\ + 64 \\ \hline \end{array}$$
$$\begin{array}{r} 17 \\ + 12 \\ \hline \end{array}$$
$$\begin{array}{r} 55 \\ + 13 \\ \hline \end{array}$$
$$\begin{array}{r} 62 \\ + \ 6 \\ \hline \end{array}$$

4.
$$\begin{array}{r} 47 \\ + 30 \\ \hline \end{array}$$
$$\begin{array}{r} 21 \\ + \ 6 \\ \hline \end{array}$$
$$\begin{array}{r} 40 \\ + 20 \\ \hline \end{array}$$
$$\begin{array}{r} 26 \\ + 53 \\ \hline \end{array}$$

Subtracting Tens and Ones

1. Subtract the **ones**.

```
    tens  ones
     4    9
  -       5
         4
```

2. Subtract the **tens**.

```
    tens  ones
     4    9
  -       5
     4    4
```

Subtract the **ones**.
Then subtract the **tens**.

1.
```
 tens ones
  5 7        2 5        8 9
 -  5       -  2       -  7
```

2.
```
  3 8        2 4        9 8
 -  5       -  1       -  6
```

3.
```
  4 7        6 6        8 9
 - 1 5      - 2 3      - 2 6
```

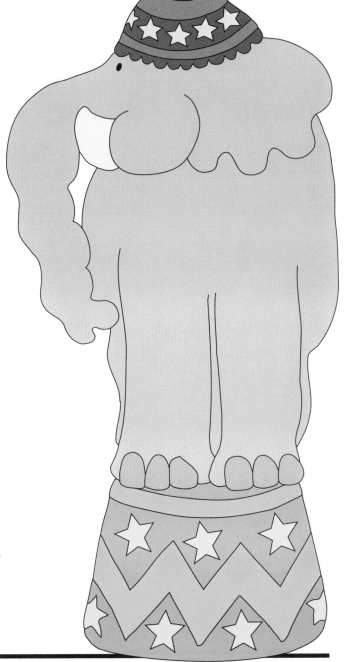

More Tens and Ones to Subtract

REMEMBER: Subtract the **ones** and then the **tens**!

1.
$$\begin{array}{r} 58 \\ -\ 36 \\ \hline \end{array}$$
$$\begin{array}{r} 77 \\ -\ 30 \\ \hline \end{array}$$
$$\begin{array}{r} 45 \\ -\ 24 \\ \hline \end{array}$$
$$\begin{array}{r} 26 \\ -\ 5 \\ \hline \end{array}$$

2.
$$\begin{array}{r} 86 \\ -\ 3 \\ \hline \end{array}$$
$$\begin{array}{r} 38 \\ -\ 17 \\ \hline \end{array}$$
$$\begin{array}{r} 67 \\ -\ 21 \\ \hline \end{array}$$
$$\begin{array}{r} 53 \\ -\ 30 \\ \hline \end{array}$$

3.
$$\begin{array}{r} 99 \\ -\ 65 \\ \hline \end{array}$$
$$\begin{array}{r} 85 \\ -\ 45 \\ \hline \end{array}$$
$$\begin{array}{r} 78 \\ -\ 4 \\ \hline \end{array}$$
$$\begin{array}{r} 37 \\ -\ 30 \\ \hline \end{array}$$

4.
$$\begin{array}{r} 48 \\ -\ 25 \\ \hline \end{array}$$
$$\begin{array}{r} 59 \\ -\ 30 \\ \hline \end{array}$$
$$\begin{array}{r} 76 \\ -\ 24 \\ \hline \end{array}$$
$$\begin{array}{r} 87 \\ -\ 3 \\ \hline \end{array}$$

Adding and Subtracting Tens and Ones

Find the **sum** or the **difference**.
Connect the dots from the **least** to the **greatest** number.

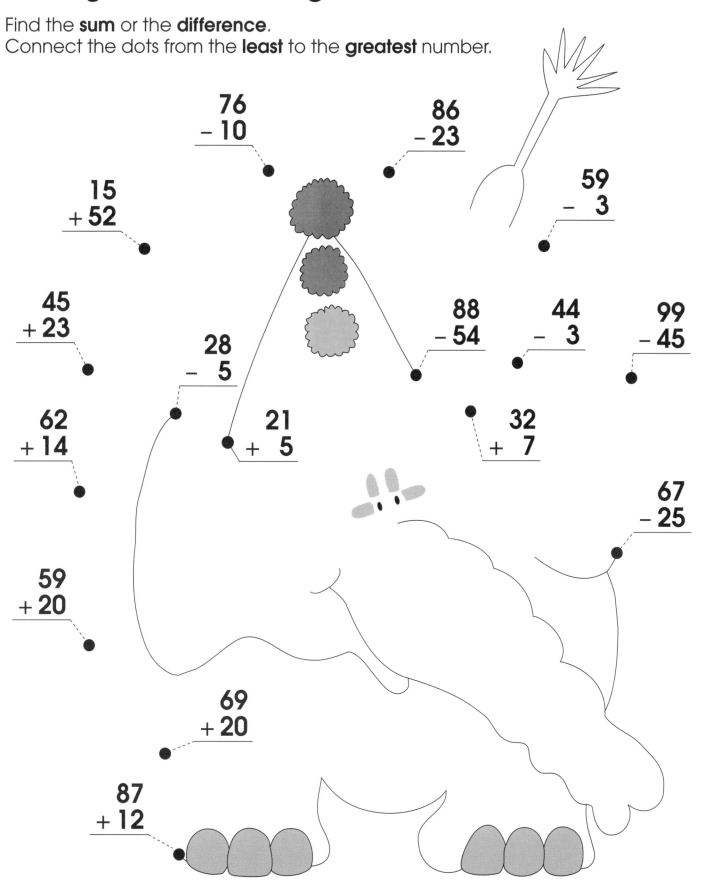

$$76 - 10$$

$$86 - 23$$

$$59 - 3$$

$$15 + 52$$

$$45 + 23$$

$$28 - 5$$

$$88 - 54$$

$$44 - 3$$

$$99 - 45$$

$$62 + 14$$

$$21 + 5$$

$$32 + 7$$

$$67 - 25$$

$$59 + 20$$

$$69 + 20$$

$$87 + 12$$

Grrrrrrrrr!

Help the lion tamer out of the cage.

$$\begin{array}{r} 6 \\ -\ 4 \\ \hline \end{array}$$

$$\begin{array}{r} 5 \\ +\ \boxed{} \\ \hline 8 \end{array}$$

$$\begin{array}{r} 9 \\ -\ 5 \\ \hline \end{array}$$

$$\begin{array}{r} 8 \\ +\ \boxed{} \\ \hline 12 \end{array}$$

$$\begin{array}{r} 9 \\ +\ 4 \\ \hline \end{array}$$

$$\begin{array}{r} 7 \\ +\ \boxed{} \\ \hline 11 \end{array}$$

$$\begin{array}{r} 12 \\ -\ 8 \\ \hline \end{array}$$

$$\begin{array}{r} 5 \\ +\ \boxed{} \\ \hline 11 \end{array}$$

$$\begin{array}{r} 12 \\ -\ 7 \\ \hline \end{array}$$

$$\begin{array}{r} 2 \\ 4 \\ +\ 5 \\ \hline \end{array}$$

$$\begin{array}{r} 9 \\ 2 \\ +\ 1 \\ \hline \end{array}$$

$$\begin{array}{r} 3 \\ 1 \\ +\ 7 \\ \hline \end{array}$$

$$\begin{array}{r} 4 \\ 7 \\ +\ 1 \\ \hline \end{array}$$

$$\begin{array}{r} 5 \\ 2 \\ +\ 3 \\ \hline \end{array}$$

$$\begin{array}{r} 9 \\ +\ 3 \\ \hline \end{array}$$

$$\begin{array}{r} 50 \\ +\ 8 \\ \hline \end{array}$$

$$\begin{array}{r} 44 \\ +\ 34 \\ \hline \end{array}$$

$$\begin{array}{r} 25 \\ -\ 2 \\ \hline \end{array}$$

$$\begin{array}{r} 66 \\ -\ 23 \\ \hline \end{array}$$

$$\begin{array}{r} 38 \\ -\ 5 \\ \hline \end{array}$$

$$\begin{array}{r} 59 \\ -\ 3 \\ \hline \end{array}$$

$$\begin{array}{r} 69 \\ +\ 20 \\ \hline \end{array}$$

$$\begin{array}{r} 76 \\ -\ 24 \\ \hline \end{array}$$

$$\begin{array}{r} 13 \\ +\ \boxed{} \\ \hline 15 \end{array}$$

$$\begin{array}{r} 4 \\ 1 \\ +\ \boxed{} \\ \hline 10 \end{array}$$

$$\begin{array}{r} 9 \\ +\ \boxed{} \\ \hline 11 \end{array}$$

$$\begin{array}{r} \boxed{} \\ +\ 5 \\ \hline 12 \end{array}$$

$$\begin{array}{r} \boxed{} \\ +\ 6 \\ \hline 12 \end{array}$$

Answer Key

Page 1
1. 2 + 2 = 4
2. 3 + 3 = 6
3. 4 + 2 = 6
4. 1 + 3 = 4
5. 1 + 1 = 2
6. 5 + 1 = 6
7. 2 + 3 = 5

Page 2
1. 6, 5, 6
2. 6, 5, 4
3. 5, 6, 6, 2, 5
4. 4, 3, 4, 5, 4

Page 3
1. 4 − 3 = 1
2. 6 − 3 = 3
3. 2 − 1 = 1
4. 5 − 2 = 3
5. 4 − 2 = 2
6. 6 − 4 = 2
7. 6 − 1 = 5

Page 4
1. 3, 3, 2
2. 1, 2, 1
3. 4, 2
4. 5, 2, 3, 1
5. 3, 1, 1, 4

Page 5
1. 6, 3
2. 2, 1
3. 4, 2
4. 6, 6, 1, 5
5. 6, 6, 2, 4
6. 4, 4, 3, 1

Page 6
1. 4, 3, 6, 5, 2
2. 6, 6, 5, 4, 5
3. 2, 1, 3, 3, 0
4. 2, 1, 0, 0, 1

Page 7

Add 1	Add 3	Add 0
5	4	6
3	6	4
1	5	1
6	3	5

Subtract 1	Subtract 0	Subtract 2
5	5	0
2	2	1
6	6	4
1	1	3

2	+ 4	**6**	− 3	**3**	− 1	**2**	+ 2	=	**4**

Elephants

Page 8
1. 3 + 4 = 7
2. 5 + 2 = 7
3. 1 + 6 = 7
4. 5 + 3 = 8
5. 7 + 1 = 8
6. 2 + 6 = 8
7. 4 + 4 = 8

Page 9
1. 7 − 5 = 2
2. 7 − 4 = 3
3. 7 − 1 = 6
4. 7 − 3 = 4
5. 8 − 5 = 3
6. 7 − 0 = 7
7. 8 − 7 = 1

Page 10
1. 7, 8, 4
2. 5, 7, 3
3. 7, 8, 6
4. 8, 5, 7, 6, 3
5. 2, 5, 8, 4, 8

Page 11
1. 7, 7, 3, 4
2. 7, 7
3. 8, 4
4. 7, 7, 5, 2
5. 8, 8, 6, 2
6. 8, 8, 1, 7
7. 8, 8

Page 12
1. 4 + 5 = 9
2. 2 + 7 = 9
3. 3 + 7 = 10
4. 8 + 2 = 10
5. 3 + 6 = 9
6. 4 + 6 = 10
7. 5 + 5 = 10

Page 13
1. 9 − 4 = 5
2. 9 − 2 = 7
3. 9 − 6 = 3
4. 10 − 8 = 2
5. 10 − 4 = 6
6. 10 − 7 = 3
7. 10 − 5 = 5

Page 14
1. 9, 9, 3, 6
2. 9, 9, 4, 5
3. 10, 10, 4, 6
4. 10, 10, 3, 7
5. 10, 10, 8, 2

Page 15
1. 6, 9, 5
2. 10, 2, 8
3. 10, 6, 9
4. 10, 10, 9
5. 3, 7, 10
6. 10, 5, 8

Answer Key

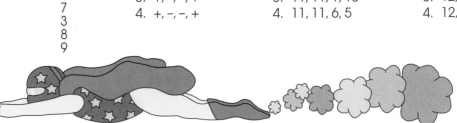

Page 16

Ladder 1	Center Clockwise from star	Ladder 2
4		10
7	10	10
2	8	7
6	3	3
9	8	8
	10	9
	9	
	3	

Page 17
1. +, −, −, +
2. −, +, −, −
3. +, −, −, +
4. +, −, −, +

Page 18
1. 11, 11, 9, 2
2. 11, 11, 7, 4
3. 11, 11, 1, 10
4. 11, 11, 6, 5

Page 19
1. 12, 12, 8, 4
2. 12, 12, 3, 9
3. 12, 12, 1, 11
4. 12, 12, 7, 5

Page 20

10	4	12	0	7	5
+ 2	+ 7	− 8	+ 9	− 3	+ 2
12	**11**	**4**	**9**	**4**	**7**
− 6	− 6	− 4	+ 2	+ 8	− 4
6	**5**	**0**	**11**	**12**	**3**
− 3	+ 5	+ 5	− 7	− 4	− 2
3	**10**	**5**	**4**	**8**	**1**

Page 21
1. 11, 9, 10
2. 12, 11, 11
3. 12, 12, 8
4. 12, 8, 12
5. 11, 10, 9
6. 7, 9, 10

Page 22
1. 5, 4, 2
2. 9, 8, 4
3. 7, 6
4. 4, 4, 5
5. 9, 5, 5
6. 6, 8, 4

Page 23

8	10	3	2	4
+ 2	− 5	+ 8	+ 6	− 3
10	**5**	**11**	**8**	**1**
− 8	+ 2	− 6	+ 3	+11
2	**7**	**5**	**11**	**12**
+ 7	+ 5	− 5	− 4	− 8
9	**12**	**0**	**7**	**4**

Riddle answer: lions

Page 24
1. 11, 12, 12, 11
2. 12, 10, 11, 12
3. 10, 12, 10, 11

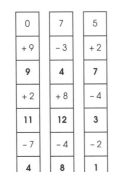

Page 25
1. 68, 97, 58
2. 73, 28, 59
3. 59, 87, 78

Page 26
1. 76, 86, 75, 68
2. 91, 97, 98, 69
3. 84, 29, 68, 68
4. 77, 27, 60, 79

Page 27
1. 52, 23, 82
2. 33, 23, 92
3. 32, 43, 63

Page 28
1. 22, 47, 21, 21
2. 83, 21, 46, 23
3. 34, 40, 74, 7
4. 23, 29, 52, 84

Page 29

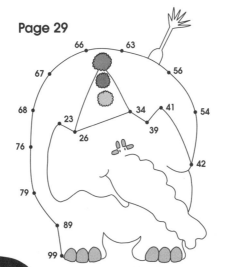

Page 30

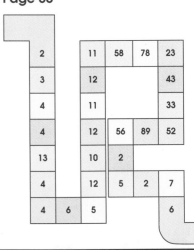